LOVE AND BASEBALL

Jerry Montoya

BROADWAY PLAY PUBLISHING INC
New York
www.broadwayplaypub.com
info@broadwayplaypub.com

LOVE AND BASEBALL
© Copyright 2011, 2023 Jerry Montoya

Cover art courtesy of Lunia Blue and The B Street Theatre

First edition: January 2023
Some text updates: August 2025
I S B N: 978-0-88145-966-1

Book design: Marie Donovan
Page make-up: Adobe InDesign
Typeface: Palatino

LOVE AND BASEBALL had a workshop production at The B Street Theatre (Buck Busfield, Artistic Director) opening on 4 March 2016. The cast and creative contributor were:

MICHELE ....Brittni Barger
WILL.. Brian Rife
Stage Manager ....Suzy Tyler

LOVE AND BASEBALL was produced by The B Street Theatre (Lyndsay Burch, Artistic Director), opening on 30 September 2022. The cast and creative contributors were:

MICHELE ....Brittni Barger
WILL.. Peter Story
Director ....Imani Mitchell
Scenic design..Samantha Reno
Costume design ....Gina Coyle
Lighting design ....Wade McKenzie-Bahr
Properties Director .... Amanda Mason
Stage Manager .... Kelsey Hammontree

CHARACTERS & SETTING

WILL, *a cameraman, aspiring filmmaker. A late bloomer who hasn't bloomed yet. Thirties, any ethnicity.*

MICHELE, *a Philosophy teacher at a local junior college. Bright, confident, fierce. Thirties, any ethnicity.*

Scene One—October. Los Angeles. A house or large apartment.

Scene Two—Two years later. Same location.

Scene Three—Two more years later. Same location.

The play is performed without intermission.

Scene One

(Unit set. The interior of a mid-sized city home. Two men live here. The living room is dominated by the television, which can be DC as the fourth wall. A sofa and two chairs face it as a shrine. A coffee table holds several remote controls. Large speakers are connected to a stereo system. The place is not as clean as WILL *would have liked it to be.)*

(As lights come up, MICHELE *enters unlocking the door with a set of keys in her hand.)*

MICHELE: I can't wait anymore. I'm letting myself in. That bathroom better be clean. Michael? Michael? Great. *(She quickly goes to the bathroom offstage into the hallway. Closes door)*

(After a moment)

*(*WILL *enters. He glances towards the television. He carries a duffel bag.)*

WILL: Mike! Why isn't the game on!? *(He sets his bag and takes his jacket off and throws them on the sofa.)* Unbelievable! Forty five takes. The last shot of the day and it took two hours longer than the five minutes it needed to be. How hard is it to say, "My name is Joe politician, and I approved this message." Two hours. I had to take a leak three hours ago. *(He makes a beeline to the bathroom. He opens the door.)*

MICHELE: Aaaaah!

WILL: Aaaaah!

MICHELE: Jesus!

WILL: Aaaaah!

MICHELE: Get Out!

WILL: Aaaaah!

MICHELE: Close the door!

(WILL *closes the door.*)

(*He backs into the living room.*)

(*Toilet flush.* MICHELE *exits.*)

(*He is standing there.*)

MICHELE: You scared the life out of me.

WILL: I am so sorry. I didn't know…are you okay?

MICHELE: I'm fine. I was startled. did you need the bathroom?

WILL: Not anymore. I think you literally scared the piss out of me.

MICHELE: You must be Will.

WILL: And you are…?

MICHELE: Michele.

WILL: That's right. Michele. The old roommate.

MICHELE: Former. Hi.

WILL: Hello. (*He takes a moment to ease his breath.*)

WILL: Is he on his way? Michael?

MICHELE: He's running late.

WILL: No surprise there.

MICHELE: I remember.

WILL: Nice to finally meet you.

MICHELE: Likewise.

WILL: How did you get in?

MICHELE: I have a key. I used to live here…

WILL: Why did you keep the key?

MICHELE: Uh, I don't know. I was going to drop it off at some point. Or throw it away. Michael mentioned once it was good someone else had it. So I kept it.

WILL: Makes sense. Just in case something happens.

MICHELE: Like you both lose your keys.

WILL: I meant something to you. So you have somewhere to go.

MICHELE: Like if I was in trouble with the law?

WILL: *(Probing)* Or your boyfriend.

MICHELE: Why would I run from my boyfriend?

WILL: I don't know you that well, I couldn't say.

(Pause)

MICHELE: You keep a bat by the door? Or is it Michael's?

WILL: It's mine.

MICHELE: In case there's a baseball emergency.

WILL: In case of an emergency of any type.

MICHELE: I see. Is that your old bat or did you buy it special? For emergencies.

WILL: As a matter of fact, I acquired that bat during an emergency.

MICHELE: Do tell.

WILL: I'm not prepared to do that at this time.

MICHELE: Sounds traumatic. Or dramatic.

WILL: A little of both actually. *(Slight pause)* So you and Michael were going to watch the game here?

MICHELE: We were going to catch a movie.

WILL: Well. That sounds like a fun date.

MICHELE: It's not a date.

WILL: Yes, ma'am.

MICHELE: I have a boyfriend.

WILL: Yes ma'am.

MICHELE: We can let go of the ma'am thing now. *(Brief pause)* You know I'm just going to… *(She turns to go, picks up her purse, moving towards the door.)*

WILL: You're leaving?

MICHELE: Well he's late and you're…awkward.

(WILL turns toward the TV and picks up a remote controller.)

WILL: Well I'll let him know you stopped in.

(MICHELE stops.)

MICHELE: You're not going to try and get me to stay?

WILL: You looked like you wanted to leave. You were leaving.

MICHELE: *(Realizing)* You want me to leave.

WILL: *(Setting the remote down)* I did not say that.

MICHELE: You didn't stop me.

WILL: I think it would be even more awkward if I tried to stop you from leaving.

(There is an awkward pause.)

MICHELE: I should go then.

WILL: *(Mumbling a bit as he turns back to TV)* It was really nice to meet you.

MICHELE: Am I being dismissed?

WILL: No. Feel free to stay if you like.

MICHELE: Thank you.

(WILL looks as if he is trying to communicate.)

MICHELE: Is there something…

WILL: I…I am trying to form a sentence that…

MICHELE: That…?

WILL: Doesn't sound as stupid as the one I am about to say.

MICHELE: Okay.

WILL: The Dodgers are in the playoffs.

MICHELE: Which one is that?

WILL: Major league baseball.

MICHELE: Yes, I am aware of that. Let me clarify. "The Dodgers are in the playoffs." Is that the stupid sentence or the rethought sentence?

WILL: I decided to go with honesty.

MICHELE: Excellent choice. Honesty has the power of economy. Do you mind if I stay?

WILL: Be my guest.

MICHELE: You can turn on the game.

WILL: I know.

MICHELE: Okay.

(Beat)

WILL: What movie were you going to see?

MICHELE: I don't know. Michael has passes to a sneak peak.

WILL: The Architect. I got the passes at work.

MICHELE: Where do you work?

WILL: Stormcrow Films. It's a production house. Commercials mainly. And if I recall, you are Michael's philosopher friend.

MICHELE: I teach a philosophy course. At City College.

WILL: Michael talks about you a lot.

MICHELE: I thought he only talked about you.

WILL: He's secretly in love with me.

MICHELE: You think Michael's gay?

WILL: No. I was just joking. Saying something…to say something.

MICHELE: One shouldn't speak unless they can improve upon the silence.

(Pause)

WILL: Point taken. I'm going to head to my room. Catch the game in there. I'm sure Michael will be here very soon.

MICHELE: You can watch the game in here.

WILL: It seems somewhat ridiculous at the moment.

MICHELE: Baseball?

WILL: No, not baseball. But watching it in here with you.

MICHELE: Oh.

WILL: So, nice to meet you. And I hope to see you again soon.

MICHELE: Do you?

WILL: *(Half a pause)* Yes.

(WILL exits. MICHELE thinks a moment or several.)

MICHELE: *(Calling to offstage)* Will?

(WILL comes back on very quickly.)

WILL: Yes.

MICHELE: What would you say to a friend if they told you they walked away from a guest to watch a baseball game?

WILL: I'd definitely tell him he was rude.

MICHELE: You might be right.

WILL: But there are other factors we have to consider.

MICHELE: Really? What other factors might there be?

WILL: Well. Three I can think of right off the bat. Michael, my friend and roommate, is on his way home to meet this woman. And two, you said you had a boyfriend. And the most pressing..

MICHELE: *(Interrupting)* I see. So if there is no chance of a hook up I have no value to you?

WILL: That's not what I intended to imply.

(Half a pause)

MICHELE: Hmmmm. What's the third factor?

WILL: Game five of the NLCS. So you see my point: there are more factors to consider other than beauty vs. game.

MICHELE: Beauty? Thank you. So what's it going to be?

(WILL makes a decision.)

WILL: Can I get you something to drink?

MICHELE: I'll get it. Kitchen still in the same place. *(She exits.)*

WILL: I'm not certain it's still a kitchen.

MICHELE: *(From offstage)* Wow. It's a disaster in here.

WILL: That's on Michael. He's a slob.

(WILL begins an epic battle to make the room as presentable as possible while he stalls MICHELE.)

MICHELE: *(She remains offstage during the following.)* You don't have any wine?

WILL: Wine? Why would we have wine?

MICHELE: It's like a micro-brewery threw up in here. Where's the thing, the opener thing?

WILL: Top drawer by the fridge.

MICHELE: Nope. That's full of soy sauce packets.

WILL: Try the bottom drawer on the left.

MICHELE: Why do you have a whole drawer full of soy sauce packets? They're not currency in this state.

WILL: They were there when I moved in.

MICHELE: Not likely. I'm not seeing it.

(WILL *knows where it is but stalls* MICHELE *as he continues to clean.*)

WILL: Try all the drawers.

MICHELE: Not finding it.

WILL: Try in the sink.

MICHELE: It's full of water.

WILL: That drain is broken. Fish around in there for it.

MICHELE: I'm not doing that.

(WILL *is on the last item to clean.*)

WILL: Maybe on top of the fridge.

(MICHELE *finds it.*)

(*She re-enters. Subtly notices the difference in the room. Hands* WILL *a beer.*)

MICHELE: I don't know how anyone can live like that.

WILL: You take the good with the bad. Thank you.

(MICHELE *and* WILL *both take a much needed drink. She looks about the room.*)

MICHELE: There was a bookshelf here.

WILL: It *might* be in the basement.

MICHELE: The basement?

WILL: Yeah. It didn't have any books on it, so we..

MICHELE: You threw it out?

WILL: Yes. Was it yours?

MICHELE: You don't own any books? *(She sets her beer down on a speaker.)*

WILL: Ummm. Let me get you a coaster.

MICHELE: Oh, I'm sorry.

WILL: No that's okay. It's just…they're speakers.

MICHELE: Big ones.

WILL: Yeah. I built them myself.

(MICHELE smiles.)

WILL: Unless you listen to recorded music on good speakers, you have not truly experienced it.

MICHELE: You've heard of these new handy little things, plays music, it's a phone, a map?

WILL: Compressed music? That's for jogging. These are for listening.

MICHELE: This is a religion.

WILL: More of a devotion.

MICHELE: *(Teasing)* This has a bit of a hipster flavor to it. But I did not sense that about you in the beginning.

WILL: Wow. You actually insulted me twice in one sentence.

MICHELE: I did not.

WILL: Yes, you did.

MICHELE: I was teasing you.

WILL: She backpedals.

MICHELE: I'm not backpedaling.

WILL: *(Clarifying)* You said I didn't look hip when you first saw me. Intimating that I am unhip. But now you get a sense of hipness and within the subtext of that discovery there was a disdainful tone.

MICHELE: Michael said you were a writer. Or was it a lawyer?

WILL: I'm a writer.

MICHELE: A writer with no books.

WILL: I have a stack in my room.

MICHELE: A whole stack?

WILL: I'm more of a film maker than a writer.

MICHELE: Another devotion?

WILL: Religion. *(He gestures to the center of the sofa.)* Sit here.

MICHELE: Why?

WILL: You need to hear these speakers.

(MICHELE ponders less than a moment. She moves to the spot.)

MICHELE: Lay it on me.

(WILL digs quickly through a pile of CDs. Or you could use a playlist from his phone.)

WILL: I would pull out the turntable but I think that might be overkill for the moment.

MICHELE: My ears are in your hands.

WILL: What type of music do you listen to?

MICHELE: Whatever is on in the background of NPR.

(WILL stands stock still for a moment and chooses to say nothing.)

MICHELE: I feel the judgement.

WILL: It was reevaluation.

MICHELE: Why am I in the middle of the room?

WILL: Sound is a wave. Simply put, sound waves need a little air to push. That's the vibration you hear. More air, the more vibration. Allowing for a much more supple sound.

MICHELE: *(Enjoying his vocabulary)* Supple.

WILL: Close your eyes. Prepare yourself. It hits hard.

(MICHELE and WILL listen. He watches her. After a bit she motions for him to stop it.)

WILL: You don't like it?

MICHELE: I do like it. I'm just, I'm feeling a little self-conscious. You're watching me listening. I can't relax.

WILL: *(Not joking)* I could leave the room.

MICHELE: That's okay.

(MICHELE's cell phone rings. She reaches into her purse to retrieve it.)

MICHELE: It's Michael.

WILL: Wait! Before you answer.

(MICHELE answers. Brackets indicate lines she is saying to WILL with her hand over the phone.)

MICHELE: Hello. [What?]

(WILL starts waving his arms to communicate "I'm not here".)

(MICHELE turns away as she talks with Michael.)

MICHELE: No. I'm fine. That's a good idea. [Stop!] I don't need anything. Junior mints.[You're going to make me laugh. Stop moving.]

(WILL freezes. MICHELE laughs.)

MICHELE: Okay. See you in a bit. *(She hangs up.)* Why didn't you want him to know you were here?

WILL: Is he on his way?

MICHELE: He's leaving in a few minutes and is going to go by a convenience store.

WILL: What for?

MICHELE: To get cheaper candy than at the movie. You didn't answer my question.

WILL: If he knew I was here he would come straight home.

MICHELE: Why would he do that and then why don't you want him to come home?

WILL: Lots of reasons.

MICHELE: You want to spend some more alone time with me and I should feel flattered…

WILL: Yes.

MICHELE: Or, Michael knows you are untrustworthy around women and would race home to save me?

WILL: You're right. Michael, that knight in shining armor.

(MICHELE *teases.*)

MICHELE: Did you want to turn on the game?

(*A quick test*)

WILL: What's your boyfriend's name?

(*Pause*)

MICHELE: Jean-Luc. And he's not my boyfriend. Anymore.

WILL: Does Jean-Luc know this?

MICHELE: Yes. He is very aware.

WILL: Earlier, you mentioned that you had a boyfriend. Now it seems you don't.

MICHELE: It seemed simpler. And not really relevant for you to know.

(*Sensing an opening*)

WILL: And the relevance has changed?

MICHELE: You asked.

WILL: What happened?

MICHELE: Things have been disintegrating for a while. I was moving out, then he was moving out. Then he got arrested.

WILL: Arrested? Drugs?

MICHELE: Embezzling.

WILL: An embezzler. Wow. So you found out and instead of breaking up you had him arrested?

MICHELE: No. His work found out. That was just…

WILL: Convenient?

MICHELE: Incidental.

WILL: And now you're dating Michael?

MICHELE: Michael? No. We're just…going to a movie. Nothing more than that. *(Pause)* I'm going to go out on a limb. See how strong it is.

(WILL waits.)

MICHELE: We can make this whatever we want it to be.

WILL: Can we?

MICHELE: Yes.

WILL: And what should we make of it?

MICHELE: What if we decided to make this a perfect first meeting? You make films, yes? If this was a movie. Right now. How would you shoot it.

WILL: What type of movie?

MICHELE: You pick the genre.

WILL: An absolute classic.

MICHELE: Yes. Strangers meet. Fate.

WILL: The perfect beginning.

MICHELE: Two people—no walls. Everything on the table. Ask any question. Tell the truth.

WILL: Any question?

MICHELE: Can you be honest?

WILL: Yes.

MICHELE: No games?

WILL: Yes.

MICHELE: That's the deal.

WILL: Is this the limb?

(Pause)

MICHELE: Are you brave?

WILL: We shall see.

(Beat. MICHELE *steps out on a limb.)*

MICHELE: What is your greatest dream?

WILL: To do something that matters.

MICHELE: Matters how?

WILL: That mean's something to people. That moves them. That makes them better people.

MICHELE: A film?

WILL: Could be.

MICHELE: What's stopping you?

*(*WILL *thinks.)*

WILL: Me. Trying to find the perfect story.

MICHELE: What makes a story perfect?

WILL: There's the rub.

MICHELE: I think that if you need a perfect story you will always be looking.

WILL: Yes. But it feels like I'm doing something if I'm looking.

MICHELE: The illusion of progress can be seductive.

WILL: It surely can be.

MICHELE: What if this becomes the perfect beginning, then...

WILL: No. Two people telling the truth. Two protagonists. No. Lacks conflict. Story is defined by conflicts. He wants this, but that is in the way. This is how he achieves it. All story is based in conflict resolution.

MICHELE: Lots of rules.

WILL: Yes.

MICHELE: Your turn to ask.

(WILL *gathers his thoughts a moment.*)

WILL: Wait. This isn't the question. I just need some back story.

MICHELE: Okay.

WILL: You've split up with your boyfriend.

MICHELE: Yes.

WILL: Of how long?

MICHELE: Almost two years.

WILL: When you moved out of here?

MICHELE: Yes. We moved in together. That's why I left.

WILL: But now he's been arrested?

MICHELE: Yes. Is that enough back story?

WILL: For now. *(Beat)* What's the worst thing to ever happen to you?

MICHELE: Looking for that conflict?

(WILL *waits.*)

MICHELE: I lost my parents very young.

WILL: How young?

MICHELE: My father when I was twelve. My mother when I was eighteen.

WILL: I'm sorry.

MICHELE: My father drank himself to death. My mother died of cancer.

WILL: Do you have any brothers or sisters?

MICHELE: A sister. Nancy. I don't know where I would be without her. *(Beat)* My parents separated. About a year before he died. My mother gave him a choice, it was either us or the drink. I used to visit him at his apartment. I'd see the bottles in his trash can. And I would think…that bottle is more important than me.

(Pause)

WILL: Are you okay?

MICHELE: I…I feel a little sucker punched.

WILL: That wasn't my intention.

MICHELE: You're a downer.

(MICHELE moves away from WILL.)

WILL: I'm more comfortable in the melancholy.

MICHELE: This was supposed to be fun and amazingly romantic.

WILL: Instead it's real. *(Beat)* I was going to offer you another beer, but…

MICHELE: I'm good, thanks.

(WILL grabs the two empties and exits to the kitchen.)

MICHELE: Have you always wanted to be a filmmaker?

WILL: *(From off)* No, that was my fallback. I wanted to be a baseball player.

MICHELE: Usually your fallback should be something more stable than film.

(WILL *re-enters*.)

WILL: That's what my Mom said. "Will, get your teaching credential."

MICHELE: Did you?

WILL: No. I didn't want anything to stop me from chasing my dreams. If I have a fallback, I'll just take it.

MICHELE: No safety net.

WILL: That's right.

MICHELE: Society has evolved because women select for stability in men.

WILL: Then marry a teacher.

MICHELE: Good advice.

WILL: Why do you only teach one class?

MICHELE: They don't hire full time professors anymore. Unless you have a Ph.D. Saves on benefits.

WILL: Bummer.

MICHELE: Hard on those student loans.

WILL: Why don't you get your Ph.D?

MICHELE: Again, hard on the student loans.

WILL: Why philosophy?

(MICHELE *laughs*.)

MICHELE: That should be a bumper sticker. Why philosophy? How much of an in depth answer do you require?

WILL: Semi-deep. Impress me.

MICHELE: Okay. I was really good at math in school. I like math. It's a language of logic. But I didn't really want to go into mathematics.

WILL: I get that.

MICHELE: And I also loved this concept from *Stranger in A Strange Land*. The Fair Witness. I wanted to be a fair witness. But that job doesn't really exist. So, philosophy came from those two things.

WILL: I don't think I read it.

MICHELE: Not surprised.

WILL: Thanks.

MICHELE: Look out the window. What color is the house across the street?

WILL: White with green trim.

MICHELE: Can you see the whole house?

WILL: Yes.

MICHELE: Or just this side?

WILL: I assume the house is painted the same on all sides.

MICHELE: That would fit with the coherence theory of truth. The correspondence theory of truth does not support that fact. A Fair Witness would answer the question thusly, the house is painted white with green trim on this side. That is the known truth of the observer.

WILL: I should have paid attention in school.

MICHELE: And listened to your Mom. "Get that teaching credential, Will."

WILL: I'll call her and tell her. She'll be thrilled.

MICHELE: How long did it take you to get everyone to call you Will? They didn't call you Will as a little boy did they? Willie?

WILL: They didn't call me Willie.

MICHELE: Was it Willie in high school or was it Will then?

WILL: William.

MICHELE: Oh no.

WILL: What?

MICHELE: It wasn't Willie. It was the other one.

WILL: Don't you…

MICHELE: Billy.

WILL: You didn't just say that.

MICHELE: Yes, I did. Billy.

(WILL *drops his head.*)

WILL: Having fun?

MICHELE: Oh, yes.

WILL: I am not just here for your entertainment.

MICHELE: I would disagree, my little Billy the clown. Did you have big old floppy clown shoes?

(WILL *gives* MICHELE *a look.*)

MICHELE: Ohh, sad clown.

WILL: We've arrived in left field.

MICHELE: Have we arrived there? Was that our destination?

WILL: Apparently.

MICHELE: Why not right field?

WILL: Right field is for kids who can't play.

MICHELE: (*She picks up a remote and points it towards the TV. She teases him.*) I wonder who's winning the game.

WILL: That's not nice.

MICHELE: If you had watched the game you would have missed out on this perfect moment.

WILL: Could be a great game.

MICHELE: Did you play?

WILL: Yes I did.

MICHELE: Were you good?

WILL: *(A qualified)* Yes.

MICHELE: Good enough to go pro?

WILL: I'd like to think so. But who knows. Tore up my knee. Badly. No more sports for me.

MICHELE: It's just a game.

WILL: I wouldn't go that far. Baseball is closer to an art than a game.

MICHELE: Baseball?

WILL: Have you ever watched a game? All the way through.

MICHELE: Guy throws ball. Guy hits ball. Running. Seemed a little random really.

WILL: It's more than just random athleticism. A great baseball game…I should say a well played ballgame is a story. Every pitch, every inning is a line of the story. It has structure, but what happens in between the lines is up for interpretation and chance.

MICHELE: I admire that you desire to romanticize the game. But ultimately, the winner of the game is determined by the inherent strength of its participants. The superior athletes win.

(WILL thinks a moment.)

WILL: Is that so? What about David and Goliath? What about Rocky and Apollo. Or what about Gibson and Eckersley.

MICHELE: Who?

WILL: Kirk Gibson.

MICHELE: Who's that

WILL: Game one. '88 World Series.

MICHELE: No idea.

WILL: They didn't teach you this in school? The 1988
World Series between the Dodgers and the "A"s.
The "A"s were the superior athletes, the best team in
baseball. The Dodgers are not even supposed to make
the playoffs. Nobody gives the Dodgers a chance to
win the Series. Nobody. The "A"s have five all-stars.
They've got the Bash brothers, Canseco and McGwire.
Steroids aren't illegal yet. But the Dodgers have a
secret weapon.

MICHELE: You.

WILL: No, no, no. Scouting. Because the Dodgers are
horrible all season. A bunch of nobodies. No one
was paying attention to them. No one scouted them
seriously until late in the season when they're already
on a roll. And that's the worst time to scout. When
a team is hot and showing no weaknesses. But the
Dodgers have been scouting the "A"s for months.
Every pitcher, every hitter. Coaching moves. All of it.
They write the book on the "A"s. They're ready. And
again, David beats Goliath.

MICHELE: Well, I guess you had to be there to
understand.

(WILL *thinks.*)

WILL: I will be needing your participation in the
following event.

MICHELE: I'm all yours. *(Beat)* Within reason.

WILL: You sit over here. You're the announcer. Vin
Scully. Can you do Vin Scully?

MICHELE: Scully? From *The X Files*?

(WILL *just stares for a moment.*)

WILL: He sounds a little like this. *(He imitates Scully.)* Get your Hoffy hot dog.

MICHELE: Get your Hoffy hot dog.

WILL: More out of the side of your mouth.

MICHELE: Get your Hoffy hot dog. Better?

WILL: It'll have to do.

MICHELE: I'm doing my best.

WILL: Stick with me. Kirk Gibson bats lefty, but I bat righty. I wish I was a switch hitter. *([Line can be cut if the actor is left-handed.] He begins to warm up his bat.)* Repeat what I say in your best Vin Scully voice.

MICHELE: *(As Scully)* Got it.

WILL: *(As Scully)* Game one of the 1988 World Series.

MICHELE: *(Repeats)* Game one of the 1988 World Series.

WILL: Ninth inning. The Dodgers are down to their last out.

MICHELE: Ninth inning. The Dodgers are down to their last out.

(WILL stops.)

WILL: This is not going to work. *(He goes to his phone.)*

MICHELE: Why not? You don't like my Scully?

WILL: It's not bad, it's just not perfect. And this is a perfect moment.

MICHELE: What are you gonna to do?

WILL: Youtube. When did you say Michael would be here?

MICHELE: About five minutes.

(WILL finds it.)

WILL: Let me fast forward. Here we go. Kirk Gibson is hurt. Can barely walk. Game one of the World Series. That's the baseball championships of the whole world.

MICHELE: The whole world?

WILL: Yes. That's what World Series means…. This isn't the whole thing. Just the at bat. So let me set it up. It's the bottom of the ninth inning. Two outs. Dennis Eckersley is pitching. Eckersley is the best closer in baseball. Hasn't given up a home run in two months. Unbeatable. The Dodgers are down 4-3. It's over. But Mike Davis comes up. Draws a walk. The tying run. And then…Gibson comes out.

(WILL *hits play on his phone. Audio of* SCULLY *begins [for copyright reasons, these are the author's words inspired by Vin Scully]. He walks out the room.)*

MICHELE: Where are you going?

WILL: I have to make my entrance.

SCULLY: And Gibson like a lion in winter comes striding out of the dugout!

(WILL *makes his entrance and has put on a ball cap or other Dodger gear.)*

WILL: Two bad knees. A pulled hamstring. He has been in the locker room all game, icing his knees. Not going to play. No way, no how.

MICHELE: This was a movie?

WILL: This actually happened. (*He practices his swing then steps into the batters box.)*

SCULLY: It's a miracle he's even walking. Both his legs are gone. Hamstring on the left and the right knee is swollen beyond recognition. I'm not sure you could even call it a knee at this point.

MICHELE: *(Unbelieving)* Come on.

WILL: Sssshhh, or I'm not going to do it.

MICHELE: Sorry.

SCULLY: I don't know if I would even take a bet on whether he can make it to first base let alone hit the ball but the Dodgers are hoping there's some magic left in that bat because it's all or nothing now!

(WILL *gets in his stance. The first pitch…*)

(*Fouled away*)

SCULLY: Eckersley looks surprised Gibson even got his bat around. As is everyone else in the stadium.

WILL: He is so banged up this is his only plate appearance in the entire series. The one and only time he bats.

SCULLY: No balls, two strikes. Two out.

(*The pitch and a swing.* WILL *hobbles to first, imitating Gibson.*)

SCULLY: Infield grounder on the line! …Foul. That looked like the most painful hobble to first I've ever seen. Gibson hasn't even been out on the field tonight. Skipped warm-ups. Skipped introductions.

WILL: Remember the Dodgers had a secret weapon.

MICHELE: Scouting.

WILL: Gibson knew…

SCULLY: Gibson shaking those legs. Trying to get the pain out. Or maybe trying to get their feeling back. Full count.

WILL: Here comes a back door slider.

(*The hit*)

SCULLY: It is high enough, is it long enough! It's gone!

(WILL *trots around the bases and does the double pump.*)

SCULLY: Gibson delivers! Dodgers win. We have all witnessed a miracle! If you weren't here to see it you might never believe it.

(WILL *stops at home. The audio ends.* MICHELE *applauds and laughs. She is charmed. He throws his cap onto the couch and sits. She picks it up and puts it on.*)

MICHELE: That might be the most darling thing I've ever seen a grown man do.

WILL: I can't believe I just did that in front of you.

MICHELE: Absolute magic. I could watch that everyday for the rest of my life.

(WILL *responds to* MICHELE's *honesty.*)

WILL: I could fall in love with you forever.

(MICHELE *takes a breath and moves away slightly.*)

MICHELE: You just met me. How can you fall in love forever?

(WILL *thinks.*)

WILL: I don't think love needs why. Love only needs love. Yes?

(MICHELE *smiles.*)

(WILL *pauses for a moment.*)

WILL: Kiss me.

MICHELE: On a first date?

WILL: This is a moment. Not a date.

MICHELE: Well, then I'm asking you on a date. What are you doing tomorrow?

WILL: (*He pauses as he realizes*) Tomorrow. Leaving.

(MICHELE *laughs.*)

MICHELE: Because I didn't kiss you?

WILL: No. For work. I leave tomorrow. I'm shooting a documentary on Mexican gray wolves. There's only eleven left. All in captivity. In New Mexico.

(MICHELE *is slightly taken aback.*)

MICHELE: For how long.

WILL: Six months.

MICHELE: Well, that poses a conundrum.

WILL: Come with me.

MICHELE: I can't do that. I have my work.

WILL: They'll get a substitute.

MICHELE: A substitute philosophy teacher? Not by tomorrow.

WILL: C'mon, it's community college.

MICHELE: What does that mean?

WILL: They're not listening anyway. Who cares?

MICHELE: I care.

WILL: That didn't come out the way I meant it. Of course you care. I just mean, there's only eleven of these wolves. There will be more kids who will come along for Philo 101.

MICHELE: I don't teach Philo 101.

WILL: My mistake. It doesn't have to be tomorrow. Come in a week or so.

MICHELE: You're serious? Just drop everything?

WILL: Are you brave?

(MICHELE *thinks.*)

WILL: I've never met anyone like you before.

MICHELE: Then don't go.

WILL: I'm making a film about the last of a breed of wolves. Extinction is permanent. It's the only time.

(MICHELE *sits down.*)

MICHELE: You might have mentioned this earlier. That you're leaving the state. Tomorrow.

WILL: It didn't seem relevant.

MICHELE: But now it does.

WILL: You asked.

(Pause. We hear a car horn from the driveway.)

(MICHELE *gets up.*)

MICHELE: That's Michael.

(MICHELE *and* WILL *stare at each other a moment.*)

WILL: We have thirty seconds. This night could be the memory of a lifetime. Our first kiss. No matter where this is going it would be an amazing memory.

MICHELE: Romantic memory insurance.

WILL: He's coming up the steps. You have five seconds. Choose.

(Blackout. Music. End of Scene)

Interstitial Section:

(During this section the set can be transformed for the next scene, pausing to focus when MICHELE *speaks.)*

(A spotlight comes up on MICHELE. *She is on the phone, one week later.)*

MICHELE: Hey there. It's Michele. Haven't heard from you. Must be a busy first week. I've got a surprise. I bought a plane ticket for Christmas break. Call me, let me know you got this. Save some wolves. Go Dodgers.

(Light go out. Music)

(Lights come back up. She is at a different spot on the stage. Later)

MICHELE: Will, hey, hope it's going well. Left you
several messages. Haven't heard back. Christmas break
is coming soon. Wondering if you can pick me up at
the airport. Or I can take a shuttle. But I need to know
where to go. Or if you'll be there. Starting to feel a little
foolish. Call me.

(Light go out. Lights back up)

MICHELE: Yes. Hello. I need to cancel my plane ticket. I
understand there's a fee. Yes, I'll hold.

(We see everything MICHELE *feels.)*

(Lights out. Music)

Scene Two

*(Two years later. It is 9 PM. Some presents on a table. It
is the night of* MICHELE's *wedding. The home has been
transformed. There is a free standing white board with a map
of all the seating for the reception drawn on it.)*

(The doorbell rings. MICHELE *comes from the bathroom
and seems incredibly busy. She charges the front door as if
everything is in a rush. She opens the door. There stands*
WILL. *He holds a gift in his hands. A small box or bag. She
stands dumbfounded. He waits.)*

WILL: Hi, there.

*(*MICHELE *gestures for* WILL *to enter. He looks around.
Taking in the place. Appreciates it. He gestures with the
gift.)*

WILL: Looks like this goes over here.

*(*WILL *takes the gift and places it on a table amongst a few
others.* MICHELE *still has not moved. Finally)*

MICHELE: Really?

WILL: I'm sorry, what?

MICHELE: Hello?

WILL: Hello.

MICHELE: Why are you in this house?

WILL: You invited me in.

MICHELE: In a larger sense. You were on the porch. It would have been rude to not…but in the grand scheme of things, why are you on my porch, now in my house.

WILL: I received your invitation. You invited me to your wedding.

MICHELE: Michael did.

WILL: And he lives here.

MICHELE: Yes.

WILL: As do you.

MICHELE: Yes.

WILL: I received an invitation to your wedding. How could I not come?

MICHELE: No RSVP.

WILL: I'm sure I sent it.

MICHELE: I'm even more sure you did not.

WILL: Maybe I forgot to mail it.

MICHELE: *(Facetious)* Maybe no stamp.

WILL: Perhaps. Is Michael here?

MICHELE: He's out.

WILL: I see.

(There is a little pause here.)

WILL: You look great.

MICHELE: Thank you.

WILL: A little angry maybe.

(MICHELE *laughs. She is busy with some preparation for the wedding.*)

MICHELE: I'm not sure "anger" is the emotion I would describe.

(*There is a pause.*)

WILL: Got anything to drink?

MICHELE: In the kitchen.

WILL: Still in the same place?

MICHELE: But now it's clean.

WILL: It wasn't me who kept it dirty. I told you that. (*He exits.*)

(MICHELE *does something to her hair to make herself a bit more presentable.*)

(WILL *re-enters with two glasses and a bottle of wine.*)

WILL: It looks like I'm your bachelorette party.

MICHELE: None for me thanks. You're not going to be here that long.

(WILL *pours one glass.*)

WILL: I would like to make a toast. (*A moment*) To second chances.

(MICHELE *drops her head.*)

MICHELE: I knew it.

WILL: (*Teasingly*) There was a moment there.

MICHELE: I can't believe it really. I let you in this house. I've only myself to blame.

WILL: Did you feel it?

MICHELE: You're deluded.

WILL: I felt it.

MICHELE: (*Sharply*) Two years. Not a word from you. I've had a speech. Carefully honed. I've spoken it to you a thousand times. Said it so many times I realized it had no meaning. That you were gone. That you never happened.

WILL: *(Cutting her off)* Before you go any further. I'm sorry.

MICHELE: Don't do that.

WILL: I am sorry.

MICHELE: Not before my speech. Don't you dare.

WILL: That's all I wanted to say.

MICHELE: Really? Sorry? Is that why you came here? Really?

WILL: Yes.

MICHELE: Thought you would show up the night before I wed. The night before. Not last week. Or next week. But right now. To say you're sorry. For what? For what are you sorry?

WILL: For not calling. For dropping out of touch.

MICHELE: For not calling? Is that what you think you needed to do? Call me? Oh, if you had only called. I wouldn't wonder what the hell happened. I wouldn't leave two or three, seven messages. Each one becoming progressively more confused. I started to feel like Alice. Watching a rabbit hole. Waiting for the bunny to come back up. Wondering if I should follow. Is he coming up? Just staring at the hole. Feeling like a fool. Because the bunny wasn't there. No more bunny.

WILL: That's a somewhat disturbing image.

MICHELE: I was disturbed. Extremely so. Deservedly disturbed.

WILL: I did wrong.

MICHELE: You did wrong. But now you're here. Why are you here Billy?

WILL: I probably shouldn't have come.

MICHELE: You made a decision to come here. You based that decision on hours. Days. Weeks of deliberating. I'm sure of it. You tried to talk yourself out if it. But you failed. Now you tell me why, Billy.

WILL: Please don't call me Billy.

MICHELE: Oh, I've called you Billy for a long time now. The farther you fell away from my memory the younger you seemed. Smaller. Adolescent. Little Billy boy, who I once mistook for a man.

WILL: Is this what you've been waiting to do? Hate me. Demean me.

MICHELE: Wait? No. You can just hear me now because you are standing close enough.

WILL: Do we really have to do this? Do you remember the first time we met?

(MICHELE stands dumbfounded.)

MICHELE: I don't think that was the right thing to say.

WILL: We talked. We made up our own rules. Michele, c'mon. I really screwed up. I know that. What could be clearer evidence than the fact that you're getting married tomorrow. I came to say I was sorry. It seemed to be more relevant to say it to you before the wedding.

MICHELE: Why didn't you come back? Or even call? What happened?

(WILL takes a deep breath. He shakes his head. Not sure how to begin.)

WILL: I…

MICHELE: No, no, no, no. You cannot play the lost little boy. You must look me in the eye. Tell me the truth. That's the deal.

WILL: *(Trying to reverse the dynamic of her questioning him)* It's nine PM. The night before your wedding. Were you just planning on spending it alone?

MICHELE: You're avoiding answering my question.

WILL: I think somewhere. I believe. You were expecting me. Tell me I'm wrong.

MICHELE: Yes, I've been sitting here like a puppy staring at the door for hours. Is he going to come home this time? What am I going to do? What a romantic view we have of oneself. You drop out for a couple years but now your back from your vision quest. My bags are all packed for a honeymoon. Perfect timing. Well done. You should go now.

(The phone rings. WILL picks it up before MICHELE can get to it.)

WILL: It's Michael calling from a strip club.

MICHELE: He's not at a strip club.

WILL: Okay. Do you want me to answer it?

MICHELE: What's the matter with you! *(She takes her phone and leaves the room. From offstage)* Hey, baby. Thanks for calling. Sounds like you're having fun. Just getting ready for tomorrow. I'm really excited too. I love you. Be safe.

(WILL stands there. Alone, he is much less sure. He wanders a little toward the door. MICHELE re-enters.)

MICHELE: Still here?

WILL: What club was he at?

MICHELE: Thinking of dropping by?

WILL: Maybe.

MICHELE: He's having drinks with friends.

WILL: I should probably stop and get some singles.

MICHELE: Is that the best you can do? Trying to make me angry at Michael for getting a lap dance. Maybe he is at a strip club.

WILL: He is.

MICHELE: Maybe he's being a little inappropriate. So what? Really. So what. Do you know how many men I've known who "pretend" they've never watched porn? Would never go to one of those juice bars? "It's weird. I get uncomfortable." We know. You are all dogs. Naked women with fake boobs are kryptonite for you.

WILL: This doesn't particularly look like you were planning a celebration to me.

MICHELE: The celebration's tomorrow. At my wedding. I'm not going to pretend to do some idiotic goodbye to my single life. I'm a grown woman. We've been living together for almost two years. I'm moving forward with my life and there's very little reason to look back.

WILL: Did you talk to Michael about us?

MICHELE: There is no us, Will. It wasn't relevant. You have no relevance to my life, do you understand? People leave. They just go.

WILL: Or you have them arrested.

MICHELE: That was incidental.

WILL: Poor Jean-Luc.

MICHELE: (*Almost a smile*) I'm okay Will. I'm happy. This is the path my life is on. Okay?

(WILL *thinks a moment.*)

WILL: I don't think I'm going to come to the wedding.

(MICHELE *smiles.*)

MICHELE: I will let the caterers know.

WILL: I guess I should go.

MICHELE: Good guess.

(WILL *turns to go. He almost gets to the door.*)

MICHELE: What was her name?

(WILL *turns.*)

WILL: I always intended to come back. I just kept getting sidetracked.

MICHELE: I'm not in a patient state of mind. What was her name?

WILL: Claire.

MICHELE: I see. Nice name, Claire.

WILL: I like it.

MICHELE: It was really that simple?

WILL: Not so simple.

MICHELE: Are you still seeing this Claire?

WILL: Yes. She's my daughter.

(MICHELE *stares at* WILL *for an extended moment.*)

MICHELE: I'm gonna need something a lot stronger than wine.

WILL: I'll get it.

(WILL *goes to the kitchen.*)

WILL: Bourbon?

MICHELE: I'm in.

WILL: Ice?

MICHELE: Just the bottle.

(WILL *enters with a bourbon bottle and two glasses. She takes one and raises it for a toast.*)

MICHELE: To Claire.

WILL: To Claire.

(MICHELE *and* WILL *drink.*)

MICHELE: I guess I should say congratulations.

WILL: Thank you.

MICHELE: Am I to assume you are the first man to have a child on his own or was there a female involved?

WILL: Her name is Moira.

MICHELE: An Irish lass. How romantic. I'm picturing red hair.

WILL: And freckles.

MICHELE: Does she know you are here?

WILL: Yes.

MICHELE: Really?

WILL: Yes.

MICHELE: Curiouser and curiouser.

WILL: We're not a couple.

MICHELE: I see. Her choice or yours?

WILL: We never really were. We tried for a time. It just wasn't meant to be.

MICHELE: Before the baby?

WILL: After we found out she was pregnant.

(Pause)

MICHELE: I have to admit. This is not what I was expecting at all. You're going to have to be tremendously more forthcoming or I am going to scream.

WILL: I flew into Albuquerque. Moira met me at the airport. She was the production manager for the documentary.

MICHELE: The wolves.

WILL: Yes.

MICHELE: It was love at first sight.

WILL: I wouldn't characterize it that way.

MICHELE: How do you want to characterize it?

WILL: I don't think I can. It was just...intense. The project was intense. We all got very close, very fast. And it just happened out of that. And then she was pregnant. And so I stayed. For Claire.

MICHELE: That was the right thing to do.

WILL: There wasn't even a question.

(MICHELE *takes it all in.*)

MICHELE: I suddenly feel very small. In comparison.

WILL: That was not my intention.

MICHELE: Is she beautiful?

WILL: An angel. *(Beat)* Forgive me.

(Beat)

MICHELE: Forgiven. *(She weeps silently.)* Billy the sad clown strikes again. Worst bachelorette party ever.

WILL: It's not too late. We could head out. Hit a club.

MICHELE: A strip club? You're joking? And what if we run into Michael?

WILL: So you do think he's at a club?

MICHELE: So what.

WILL: I could just put on a show for you here.

MICHELE: What do you mean? You'll do a strip tease?

(WILL smiles. Does a little dance)

MICHELE: Don't be childish.

WILL: I thought women like childish.

MICHELE: Childlike not childish.

WILL: That's a fine line.

MICHELE: Not really. I'm almost tempted. Just to see you humiliate yourself.

WILL: I've humiliated myself enough without the help. *(Jokingly)* So what have you been up to?

MICHELE: Oh you know, teaching, planning my wedding.

WILL: I would like to request you elaborate on that?

MICHELE: Well, after you decided to never call me back…you could have called.

WILL: I couldn't think of what to say. After a while it seemed ridiculous to even think to call.

MICHELE: Well, of all things, Michael asked me to move in after you left and never came back. We were both paying rent on a house by ourselves. Seemed like a good idea.

WILL: *(Pushing)* And you fell in love?

MICHELE: Don't do that. He's my best friend. It grew from that.

WILL: And that's it?

MICHELE: Yes. Not everyone needs a passionate fling in an airport lobby to fall in love.

WILL: It wasn't that fast.

MICHELE: Pretty fast.

WILL: Yes. Pretty fast.

MICHELE: And what? It just didn't work out between you?

WILL: *(Pointedly meaning her)* I was in love with someone else. She knew that. I told her that.

MICHELE: *(Shaking her head)* You are a peach.

WILL: Ty Cobb ain't got nothing on me.

MICHELE: Whatever that means I'm sure I agree.

WILL: You don't know who Ty Cobb is?

MICHELE: Some other jackass?

WILL: An old time baseball player. Probably the best ever. Arguably.

MICHELE: I don't see the connection.

WILL: They called him the Georgia Peach. It was meant ironically. He was a bit of an asshole.

MICHELE: I see the connection now. Why don't you make a movie about baseball?

WILL: Seriously? Eight Men Out. The Natural. Field of Dreams. It's been done. Very well.

MICHELE: How about a documentary?

WILL: You're kidding me right?

MICHELE: Been done?

WILL: Definitively. Believe you me, if I had a baseball story, I'd tell it.

MICHELE: The documentary about the wolves. How'd it turn out?

WILL: Good. Pretty good. It might get sold to National Geographic.

MICHELE: That's nice.

WILL: I won't get any more money if it does but..

MICHELE: Good exposure.

WILL: Yes.

MICHELE: Were you happy with it?

WILL: I'm too critical.

MICHELE: And the wolves, extinct?

WILL: Not yet.

MICHELE: Do you have a picture? Of your daughter. Claire.

WILL: I do. Would you like to see it?

MICHELE: *(She nods.)* I didn't at first. I'm ready now.

(WILL takes out his phone and brings up a photo.)

WILL: Meet Claire.

MICHELE: She's adorable.

WILL: Are you..and Michael…

MICHELE: *(Waving her finger no-no)* These are not questions you get to ask.

WILL: Really?

MICHELE: Really.

WILL: I see.

MICHELE: And you don't get to make silent assumptions either.

WILL: Yes, ma'am. You should open your present.

MICHELE: Ah, yes, your gift. *(She retrieves it. She shakes it.)* Should I guess?

WILL: If you like.

MICHELE: Feels like a rock.

WILL: No.

MICHELE: A massive diamond?

WILL: No.

MICHELE: Your cold dead heart?

WILL: Strike three.

(MICHELE opens it. It is a new baseball in a box.)

MICHELE: Very cute.

WILL: I signed it and everything.

(MICHELE takes it out of the box to read it.)

MICHELE: I should throw this at you.

WILL: If you wish.

MICHELE: Remember the first time we met? That was a dumb question.

WILL: Are you reminiscing?

MICHELE: Don't ruin it.

WILL: Sorry.

MICHELE: Or apologize.

WILL: Okay.

MICHELE: Before you go. Do the baseball thing again.

WILL: Why?

MICHELE: It's childlike. It's how I want to remember you.

WILL: You're serious?

MICHELE: Yes.

WILL: The Kirk Gibson homerun?

MICHELE: No. A different one.

WILL: Gibby hit a big one for the Tigers too. It's a funny one. You could be Sparky Anderson this time. "They don't want to walk ya!"

MICHELE: I don't want to be Sparky.

WILL: I don't blame ya. Are you sure you want a baseball story?

MICHELE: The second time we've met and you're already out of stories.

WILL: Give me a sec. This is our second date?

MICHELE: No comment.

WILL: The number two in baseball... The number two in baseball... It's a number that means you are on the edge. Two outs. You only get two strikes. A double play. There's few things in sports as beautiful as a double play. It takes a batter less than four seconds to get to first base. That's all the time you get. The fielder used to just be able to drag his foot near the base and not actually touch it. *(He figures it out. Excited)* I've got it. The Merkle Boner.

MICHELE: The..

WILL: Merkle.

MICHELE: Boner. Is that your story?

WILL: One of the most controversial games in baseball history. And I believe it has a certain relevance. Ready for this?

MICHELE: Let's say yes.

WILL: So this was a long time ago. Early 1900s. The Cubs and Giants are playing at the Polo Grounds in New York. They're in the pennant race. The winner of which goes to the World Series. With me?

MICHELE: No.

WILL: Two teams. Very important game.

MICHELE: Got it.

WILL: It's the ninth inning. Two outs. Giants are batting. The game is tied. One to one. *(He uses the room as his field. Places a pillow on a chair for third.)* There's a runner on third base. *(Places the white board in the proper position to be second base.)* And this is important, there is absolutely no one on second. *(Places a pillow on a chair for first.)* And there's a runner on first. This is the aforementioned Merkle. Remember the game is tied, one to one. If the runner on third scores, the Giants win.

MICHELE: Same as in kickball.

WILL: Absolutely. Same as in kickball. Giants batter steps up. The pitch. Crack! He smashes the ball into the outfield. The runner on third races home. The crowd goes wild, they storm the field. Pandemonium! Giants win!

MICHELE: That's it? Game's over? That's a horrible story.

WILL: This is baseball. This is the beauty of the game. Nothing ever happens the way you expect it to happen. From perfect order can come chaos. The game is not over because there was no force out.

(MICHELE *raises her hand.*)

WILL: You don't have to raise your hand.

MICHELE: Sorry, force out?

(WILL *erases the white board on which* MICHELE *has attempted to organize the seating arrangement for the wedding. She is not pleased. He draws on it to explain the following.*)

WILL: Right, a force out is when you are forced to go to the next base because the batter has to take the base you're on after they hit. Now if the opposing team catches the ball on the base you're headed to *before* you get there you are… Forced out.

MICHELE: Forced out.

WILL: And if there is a force out then the run doesn't count.

MICHELE: Got it.

WILL: So, remember Merkle is on first base. The ball is hit, Merkle is now *forced* to run to second because the batter is *now* a baserunner. But when he sees his teammate score, he stops. He stops. "We won. We won." And then Merkle turns and runs straight to the locker room. He never touches second.

MICHELE: Then the game isn't over! The ball is…

WILL: Alive and kicking. And the second baseman sees that Merkle doesn't touch second.

MICHELE: And if Merkle is out at second the run doesn't count.

WILL: Boom. So the second baseman starts screaming to the outfielder "throw me the ball! Throw me the ball!"

MICHELE: Oh my god!

WILL: Remember there's people all over the field celebrating. So the outfielder has to run through them all, he then finds the ball. He turns, he throws it…..and it is intercepted by the Giants first base coach who saw the whole thing happening.

MICHELE: He can't do that!

WILL: Pandemonium. He intercepts the ball and turns and chucks it into the stands.

MICHELE: No!

WILL: Yes! And so the Cubs players climb into the stands looking for the ball. Finally someone finds it, they throw it to the second baseman, who ever so casually steps on second. You're out Merkle. Ya bonehead.

MICHELE: So the game is still tied.

WILL: Exactly. And now it's too dark to finish and the crowd is all over the field so they had to play the entire game again two weeks later. And this time the Cubs won. *(Pause)* So it just goes to show, you never know what can happen if you get a second chance.

(MICHELE *takes a moment.*)

MICHELE: And that's what you think you deserve? A second chance.

WILL: Well, the Cubs did go on to win the World Series.

(MICHELE *crosses to* WILL.)

MICHELE: You're not the Cubs in this story Will. You're Merkle. It was right in front of you but you turned and ran. You blew it, ya bonehead.

WILL: Well, then I'm glad I'm not the Cubs, cause they had to wait a whole 'nother hundred years to win a World Series. I definitely was not waiting that long.

MICHELE: The Merkle boner. You're right, I shouldn't have chosen a baseball story.

WILL: If you like I will give you a second chance. This is your movie moment. You can make of it whatever you want.

MICHELE: How about you do The Invisible Man.

WILL: A classic horror. Not what I expected. But intriguing.

MICHELE: *(She ponders.)* Okay. Then dance. To dance with me. Like in a movie.

WILL: *Dirty Dancing*?

MICHELE: Nice try but no. Tango. Do you dance?

WILL: No.

MICHELE: Such a shame.

WILL: You tango?

MICHELE: No, but I took some dance classes back in the day.

WILL: You're serious?

MICHELE: If I am are you really going to dance with me?

WILL: Sure.

MICHELE: I'm serious.

(WILL *bows and offers his hand.*)

WILL: Do you have any tango music.

MICHELE: Just choose something. We can tango to anything. It will be easier if it's something you know.

(WILL *looks through the CDs or her phone or whatever. They move the coffee table and clear any glasses.*)

MICHELE: I'm nervous.

(WILL *turns to* MICHELE.)

WILL: Neither one of us can dance the tango. It's okay. Let's just dance.

MICHELE: Okay. Let's first start by figuring out the first position.

WILL: Without the music?

MICHELE: Just the first pose.

WILL: Okay.

(MICHELE *and* WILL *face each other.*)

MICHELE: Okay. This hand like this.

(MICHELE *puts* WILL'*s left hand into her right hand.*)

MICHELE: I put my hand on your shoulder. Your hand goes here. Okay?

WILL: Yes.

(MICHELE *pauses.*)

MICHELE: Will. This dance. Then I never see you again.

(WILL *nods.*)

(MICHELE *disengages and starts the music. Music begins. They move into their first position. They listen. He leads as best as he can. She follows. They slowly find their rhythm. He dips her. She laughs. He moves her around the room. He spins her away from him. She spins back. They are not amazing dancers but they find each other and play. He dips her.)*

WILL: I wish I was a better dancer.

MICHELE: You are perfect.

(MICHELE and WILL continue dancing for a moment. They are close and move well together.)

(It begins to grow too close.)

(She decides to end the dance. She shuts off the music.)

(She turns away to recover.)

(They take a moment. They are both breathing a little heavily.)

(He turns and begins to leave but stops.)

WILL: I really do love you.

(Beat)

MICHELE: I'm getting married tomorrow.

(WILL nods and exits. MICHELE stands for a moment. Lost)

(Music. Blackout)

(End Scene)

(WILL changes into slightly more formal attire then steps into a spotlight. He hold an award in his hand.)

WILL: Thank you. First to the National Academy of Television Arts and Sciences. This is a tremendous honor. It was my privilege to work on Desert Wolves. I would like to especially thank my producing partner Moira Kelly, and my daughter Claire, who has made my life so much more full. By definition a documentary is attempting to create a record. We are informing but also marking the time. A signpost that says, this was important and we missed it. Maybe. I was inspired by these wolves, back from the brink of extinction, that the end may not be the end. Sometimes what's seems so improbable surprises you, and becomes the possible. You just need to be brave.Thank you. (*He exits.*)

Scene Three

(*Two years later than Scene Two.* MICHELE *is now picking up the pieces from a failed marriage and is packing to leave this house. There are boxes about the room and the place is half packed. As much furniture as possible is out of the room.*)

(MICHELE *enters from the front door, she wears earbuds and is talking to her sister on the phone. She brings in an empty hand truck. She wears work gloves and moving clothes that are loose and while not scanty, eventually she will feel the need to wear slightly more. She speaks as she enters. The door is left partially open.*)

MICHELE: I don't think he really cares. I'm packing up the truck now. I'm going to be out of here tonight. The rest is his. I don't know. He'll probably sell it all in a garage sale. No. He won't be back for a couple of days.

(WILL *has entered the slightly opened door.*)

(MICHELE *has picked up a box and turns towards the door.*)

(*She sees* WILL. *She is startled and drops the box which makes a loud crash.*)

MICHELE: Mother of…

WILL: My apologies. I should have knocked.

(MICHELE *signals for him to be silent. Finger across lips and shaking her head.*)

(*She continues on the phone.*)

MICHELE: Nancy. I'm going to have to call you back. No, I'm fine. I just found something disgusting Michael left behind. I'm going to have to clean it up and throw it out. Yeah. Bummer. Okay. Love you. (*She hangs up.*)

WILL: Subtle. I was in the neighborhood. Saw the truck. Thought maybe you might need some help.

(MICHELE gestures again for silence.)

(She slowly begins to walk in a large circle around WILL. He watches her.)

(She gathers her thoughts.)

MICHELE: Like a pox you are. A virus. You keep mutating. I think I've beaten you and there are months, years of health. But then…then…a what do you call it…what's the word…

WILL: Relapse?

(MICHELE gestures again for silence.)

MICHELE: You relapse. Fever. Delusions. I must be having a delusion. Because there is no possible reality in which during the process of packing my belongings in the midst of a very bitter divorce from an even briefer infection I called a marriage, would it even be possible that you would walk in and stand in the middle of my living room. I'm at a loss.

WILL: If you'd let me…

(Again the gesture to be silent)

MICHELE: No. *(Pause)* Do you ever become men? Or are you just boys who get older?

(Pause)

WILL: May I answer?

MICHELE: Yes.

WILL: Are you referring to me or to your husband?

(MICHELE moves to begin packing her boxes.)

MICHELE: Who I'm divorcing because I thought I married a man. Only to discover that what I married wanted me to be his nanny.

WILL: His dirty nanny.

MICHELE: Don't do that.

WILL: Sorry.

MICHELE: Are you really here?

WILL: I'm sorry things didn't work out with Michael.

MICHELE: Am I supposed to believe that?

WILL: Well, I don't see…

MICHELE: Are you going to answer any questions tonight?

WILL: Yes.

MICHELE: Then let me ask you this. Why don't boys become men? Why can't you show love? Why are you all so angry and insecure? Why the sex hang-ups? Why must you stare at naked women as much as possible every single day? Why can't you stop being selfish, rude, dirty, sloppy children?

WILL: We need a lot of praise, you need to praise us more.

MICHELE: For what?

WILL: Everything. We haven't evolved as a species very far from the caveman. Houses, cars, computers, these things are recent and they have come fast. They mean nothing in evolutionary time. We no longer get the adoration that is inherent in capturing and slaughtering a mastodon, so what we need is constant praise.

MICHELE: Even if you've done nothing?

WILL: *(Resolutely)* Yes.

(MICHELE *ponders.*)

MICHELE: And if you've actually done something?

WILL: Double the praise.

MICHELE: This feels true.

WILL: *(Reminding her to praise)* You should say, "This feels true. Good answer."

MICHELE: *(She reluctantly praises him.)* Good answer. It's that easy?

WILL: Absolutely.

MICHELE: *(Closes her eyes)* I'm seeing waves and waves of relationships gone bad, break-ups flying through my head…I've watched dozens of rejected men cry as I fail to praise their simple existence…

(MICHELE hurls something at WILL.)

MICHELE: Be responsible for your own happiness!

WILL: I'm sensing anger.

MICHELE: Oh, Mr Aloof. Mr Big Shot. Congratulations by the way.

WILL: You saw me win it?

MICHELE: Online. You gave a nice little speech. Your parents must be proud.

WILL: They are. Congratulations yourself. Tenure track. Impressive.

MICHELE: Thank you. Like crawling through glass to get there. I heard you were back living in LA.

WILL: Is that what you heard?

MICHELE: And dating some B-List actress.

WILL: Spending a lot of time online these days?

MICHELE: It's what those who are in the process of divorce have to do. No one wants us around. After the divorce we can re-integrate. During, it's awkward.

WILL: You shouldn't believe everything you read.

MICHELE: Is that so?

WILL: And at her age, it's not B List. It's "up and coming."

MICHELE: *(Mocking)* She must be proud.

WILL: It wasn't a big thing.

MICHELE: I see. And your show at the gallery. Michael was a little hurt to not be invited.

WILL: Not invited? It was at the Brickhouse. It's an Art Gallery. Open to the public.

MICHELE: Is that what we are? Your public? And I meant an invitation to the opening. Michael wanted to go to the opening.

WILL: Maybe next time.

MICHELE: I didn't know you were a painter.

WILL: It was photographs. Photos of the wolves. I filmed them but I also shot a lot of stills.

MICHELE: Oh.

WILL: You thought I was a painter? How romantic of you. Did you fantasize about me? Painting in my studio. Shirt off. Dirty painter pants.

MICHELE: Clearly that is your fantasy of what you think is sexy.

(WILL chuckles.)

MICHELE: So are you now working on saving some other animal from extinction?

WILL: My agent kept me pretty busy for a while.

MICHELE: Your agent. Fancy. Things slowing down?

WILL: Just going in a new direction.

MICHELE: What a surprise.

WILL: You are on some type of mean pills today.

MICHELE: It's been a difficult time.

WILL: I can imagine.

MICHELE: I don't think you can.

WILL: Fair enough. I'm actually back at my old job.

MICHELE: Kind of a step backwards.

WILL: I'm actually a partner there. Took the proceeds from my recent work and purchased half the business. It's not glamorous. Commercials, industrials, mainly. Good, solid and steady.

MICHELE: Not chasing the dream anymore?

WILL: I chase her every day. And when I catch her she laughs and laughs. Claire. She's the dream now.

MICHELE: How is she?

WILL: She's doing great.

MICHELE: Do you see her often?

WILL: All the time. She lives with me now.

MICHELE: Here in LA?

WILL: Moira and I bought a duplex. She in one. I, the other.

MICHELE: How very adult.

WILL: Being in New Mexico wasn't going to help me in my career. Moira agreed to move. After I hired her.

MICHELE: So she's the mother of your child and you're her boss?

WILL: I'm really enjoying it. Her, not so much.

MICHELE: I would imagine.

WILL: It's actually fine. We co-parent well. Eyes on the prize.

MICHELE: I'm impressed.

WILL: And you?

MICHELE: And me what?

WILL: You're moving?

MICHELE: Yeah. Well.

(MICHELE *doesn't know what to say and* WILL *doesn't press.*)

WILL: Is Michael still living here?

MICHELE: He will be out by the end of the week.

WILL: Sad to see it go. I have a lot of great memories here.

MICHELE: *(Pointed)* Why are you here Will?

WILL: Because I missed you.

MICHELE: Now is not a good time for me Will.

WILL: I understand.

MICHELE: I know it might seem like I have a tremendous amount of control but, in all honesty, I'm about to meltdown right about now.

WILL: *(Moves to her, trying to soothe her)* It's okay.

(MICHELE *stops* WILL *with a gesture.*)

MICHELE: No. Just silence for a moment. Maybe a full minute.

WILL: Silence for one minute?

MICHELE: Yes. *(She backs away. And then begins to feel a little self conscious. She has been wearing "moving clothes.")* I'm feeling a little exposed. I'm going to uh… *(She grabs a box and heads to the kitchen.)* Do you want anything to drink?

WILL: Whatever you're having. Thank you. *(He grabs a box. Tapes it up. Moves it to the hand truck. Maybe picks up the box she dropped. Shakes it. Broken dishes. Moves it to the side)*

(MICHELE *enters and is wearing a San Francisco Giants jersey which she pointedly models for* WILL.)

(She has two bottles of water.)

WILL: Nice jersey.

MICHELE: You inspired me to become a baseball fan. And there's nothing I love more than watching the Dodgers lose.

WILL: Next year.

MICHELE: What's Claire's size? I'll get her one.

WILL: She doesn't wear diapers any more.

MICHELE: I'd like to meet her.

WILL: I would like that.

MICHELE: We'll make sure it happens soon.

WILL: How about dinner tomorrow?

MICHELE: I'm pretty sure I'm not ready for that.

(Beat)

WILL: Was it bad?

(Beat)

MICHELE: Yes.

WILL: I'm sorry.

MICHELE: Me too.

WILL: Someone else?

MICHELE: Just a bottle. Maybe there was someone else but he wouldn't remember if there was.

WILL: Michael?

MICHELE: He drinks. Didn't you know that? I didn't realize how much or how often. Neither did he apparently.

WILL: AA?

MICHELE: I gave him the choice. He made the same decision as my father.

WILL: That must have hurt.

MICHELE: C'est la vie. *(Abruptly)* You know, I'm really surprised to say this but it was good to see you. Thanks for stopping by.

(MICHELE begins to pack again. WILL gets up to go.)

WILL: Let me help you get this stuff into the truck.

MICHELE: You don't need to do that.

WILL: I know. I want to. *(He has moved and picked up a box to carry outside.)*

MICHELE: *(Trying to stop him)* Will. Will. Will!

(WILL sets the box down and is a bit stunned by MICHELE's fury.)

(She recovers a bit.)

MICHELE: While our lives have a maddening tendency to collide every few years, they are not intertwined. I have not been pining for you. There are no open arms waiting for you. You have made your choices and I have made mine. We actually don't really know each other. We can pretend that it was something else but it really wasn't.

WILL: I totally get why you would say that. I do. But, as you may recall, last couple times we saw each other..

MICHELE: It was just the two times.

WILL: Are you sure it was just two?

MICHELE: Absolutely positive.

WILL: Then you will recall we set the bar at honesty. And I'm telling you, I'm not here to attempt to rekindle some type of anything.

(MICHELE thinks. And then ponders over it. Her guard drops a little. She trusts WILL's word.)

MICHELE: I'm not here to attempt to rekindle some type of anything. Are you going to stand by that?

WILL: It wasn't great sentence structure, I would agree. But the sentiment was clear.

MICHELE: It was. So. If it was not your intention to "rekindle" some type of...

(WILL joins in.)

WILL: Type of anything.

MICHELE: Then why are you here?

(WILL takes a moment.)

WILL: I'm sorry. I have to be honest, I'm nervous.

MICHELE: I hadn't noticed.

WILL: I'm getting pretty good at hiding it. I seem to spend most of my time in meetings these days. Lots of practice. I want to answer your previous question in a slightly different way. I don't think we ever grow up. On the inside. We are really children. We are all so new. Watching Claire become this amazing, charming little person I am left in so much wonder. And why I am here is that the only thing that makes me sad anymore is I can't share those moments with you. I know that sounds ridiculous. But I met this person that is you so many years ago and I was a fool then. I'm not one anymore. I'm not asking for anything other than friendship. I give you my word on that.

(MICHELE thinks.)

MICHELE: You have learned to handle that nervousness quite well.

WILL: Thank you.

(Beat)

MICHELE: We set the bar at honesty.

WILL: That we did.

MICHELE: I would really love to take you up on this amazing offer of friendship.

WILL: Great.

MICHELE: But I can't. I just can't.

(A slight moment as WILL takes that in.)

WILL: I get it. It was a pleasure to see you again. Sincerely. *(He turns to go. He gets to the door.)*

(MICHELE is slightly stunned.)

MICHELE: You're just going to walk out?

WILL: I thought you wanted me to leave.

MICHELE: And that's it?

WILL: You very politely refused my offer of friendship. It's a fair assumption you wanted me to go.

MICHELE: Let me explain.

WILL: I'm not owed an explanation. I'm not arguing with you.

MICHELE: Why not?

WILL: *(He searches briefly.)* Respect.

MICHELE: Thank you.

WILL: No problem. I can take a strike three. But I wasn't going to take strike three looking.

MICHELE: But I would like to explain.

WILL: I'm all yours. *(Beat)* Within reason.

(MICHELE smiles. And is released)

MICHELE: You know, you're right. I don't need to explain.

(MICHELE walks away and continues to pack. WILL then turns to go.)

MICHELE: I can't do dinner tomorrow. How about next week? Wednesday?

(WILL stops. He is ecstatic but covering it.)

WILL: Dinner next Wednesday it is.

MICHELE: I am excited to meet Claire.

WILL: She will be excited to finally meet you.

MICHELE: You've mentioned me to her?

WILL: Well. I tell her stories some times…I just make them up now and again. And the princess is almost always named Michele.

MICHELE: *(Maybe briefly touched then comes to her senses)* What's the prince's name?

WILL: Fred.

MICHELE: Just checking.

WILL: I get it.

MICHELE: Thank you.

WILL: No problem.

MICHELE: Is it absolutely necessary that you always have the last word?

WILL: No.

MICHELE: Then stop.

WILL: Okay.

MICHELE: C'mon.

WILL: You c'mon.

MICHELE: I will scream if you say another word.

(Beat. WILL raises his hand.)

MICHELE: You in the back with your hand up. You have a question?

WILL: Thank you. I just want to clarify. Do you mean if I say "another word". Or actually any other word?

MICHELE: I think I'm done for the night. I'm beat and I need to finish.

WILL: Sure you don't want my help?

MICHELE: Yes. I need to do this on my own. But next Wednesday. And yes, it would be nice to see you now and again.

WILL: Great. Monday and Wednesdays starting in the fall.

(MICHELE *realizes.*)

MICHELE: You didn't?

WILL: Signed up for your class, very excited.

MICHELE: *(Not threatened)* I think they call that stalking.

WILL: I would have dropped the class if this hadn't gone well.

MICHELE: No one drops my class.

WILL: Yes ma'am.

(WILL *turns to go as* MICHELE *preps another box. She finds his wedding gift baseball inside.*)

MICHELE: Will?

(MICHELE *holds up the baseball.* MICHELE *and* WILL *look at each other.*)

WILL: Every time?

MICHELE: I think that's our tradition. Before you leave you must tell me a baseball story. Third time's the charm.

WILL: This is a bad precedent.

MICHELE: The precedent has already been set.

WILL: Okay. Give me a moment. Three's not a great number in baseball.

MICHELE: Three strikes. Three outs. Three balls is good.

WILL: I have no response to that. But there is a specific situation where three is a very good number.

MICHELE: And when is that?

WILL: When you're on third base.

MICHELE: And that's where we are?

WILL: This is our third date. You see, it doesn't matter how we got here. Because here we are. Standing on third.We hit that third strike deep into the corner. Stretched a double into a triple. Or maybe we just hit a little squibber down the line and sneaked onto first when the throw was wide. Took second on a passed ball. Got to third on a balk. We haven't even earned it. But on third we are.

MICHELE: And what does that get us?

WILL: It's what happens next that matters. 1955 World Series. Dodgers and Yankees. Game one. The great Jackie Robinson is standing on third base. In the house that Ruth built. And no one in the entire stadium could even imagine it. But you know what Jackie was thinking?

MICHELE: Steal home.

(Music. MICHELE goes to WILL and kisses him.)

(Fadeout)

END OF PLAY